AF408264

3

the graveyard within me

a poetry collection by Anne Pyle

this book explores heavy topics such as:
- emotional control & neglect of a child
- verbal & psychological abuse
- harmful family members
- pedophilia, incest & ableism
- generational trauma
- trauma triggering/being triggered
- fear and terror

please make sure you are in a safe, stable headspace before continuing.

table of contents

but the flowers, ii

flowers so vibrant I scarcely seem to exist.
a soft sunbeam carrying a muggy warmth.
dogs prowling in streets, so loud for attention.
but the flowers.
ignore the silence. ignore
the violent decor and browning grass.
focus on the Indian paintbrushes,
the swaying bluebonnets composing the hill.
walk beside the flowers and try,
try to imagine a complex time when
you were consumed by stress. you were made of worry
and you ran and you ran and you ran.
stop walking and sit. large grasshoppers
cling at every leaf, clueless and abundant.
the dogs walk past you.
you pretend you never were.

part one
the graveyard

"i love you"

over two decades of being invisible,
of pretending to be his best friend,
tucking behind fake smiles,
being Daddy's little girl,
calling twice a year,
forcing myself to
ignore the truth
right in front
of my face,
pretend it
was okay
so that I
could
hear
him
say
it.

I want to make my bed
just how you would like it.

cover my pillows up
with ornamental cushions.

blanket folded over
just enough to draw the eye in.

I added my own flair,
a childhood heirloom bear,

and burst into tears
thinking of all the years I lost

because I didn't know
you didn't know.

reversing everything I said,
ignoring everything you did,

I want to hold onto you
one last time,

erase the decade of silence,
and tell you how much I love you.

big bad bob

waking up on Saturday to
the stinging odor of burnt food
made me run down the stairs
because it meant Daddy's home.

I never minded the taste
of the blackened breakfast
or the hot dog char,

because he cared enough
to grace us with his presence.

if he screamed at us,
we failed him somehow.
if he ignored us for days,
he was just busy with work.

so I accommodated for him.
I made excuses for his tardiness
or absence to every school event.

as reward, he shirked out of loans
he promised Mom he'd pay.

new kids, new wife, new car,
new house, new pets, new life,
new scapegoats for everything
he didn't care to give attention.

out of all the hurtful things
he did and said to us as kids,
nothing stung quite like that.

he forgot about the bacon, the burgers,
the ball games, the bank accounts, the bills,

and me.

premonition

the most painful part of
having you for a dad
is remembering times
you didn't disgust me.

you're an abuser,
and a psychopath,
and a pedophile,
and yet I'll admit:

I used to look for you
in a crowd, hoping
you were there, waiting
for you to show up.

you were flirting with
my closest friends at
my eleventh birthday
party, but I didn't know.

I was just happy
you were spending
time with me. back then,
I thought you loved me.

sometimes I'll listen to
one of your favorite bands,
or recall an inside joke
we used to giggle about,

or some snack you liked
and I'd start liking it too,
just so it could become
our secret little treat.

I wish these fond memories
made me happy, like everyone
else does when their dads
still care about them.

instead, they sting with guilt,
like I should've caught on
instead of being a normal kid
who wants her dad to love her.

but you hated me instead,
didn't you?

sunday best

I stay up so, so late,
obsessively organizing my family tree.

I scour a hundred years
of history, looking for something, anything.

my great-grandparents,
immigrants seeking a better life without poverty.

my great aunt,
a physician and director of a methadone clinic.

my grandmother,
the only daughter with five younger brothers.

corrine said
her father forced her to wear skirts.

even after she married and
moved hundreds of miles away, she obeyed him.

but from when he died
until the day she was buried,

she wore pants every day.

I hope that when they put her in the ground,
she was wearing her favorite outfit.

hair straightened, perfume spritzed,
blouse ironed, jewelry polished,

and her most precious pair of pants
starched just for her.

guilt trip

you told me:

Dad disliked me
because I was too much
like his mother.

you told me:

I have to get skinnier
because I was getting fat
and you were just
worried about my
health,
that's all.

you told me:

you read my books
and always knew I was
your most gifted child.

you told me:

you went to counseling,
and you're better now,
and you're proud of me,
and you're
so, so
sorry.

I tell you:

you're a really good liar,
but I don't need to
believe you anymore.

big brother

while he stands there, telling me
disturbing sex acts he's done
until I feel horrified and sick;

as he insists my loving husband
is an abuser, manipulating me
in everything he is and does;

when he claims nothing's wrong,
I'm taking it out of context,
and being stupid, and emotional:

he just keeps smiling.

he gets everything he wants.
he's the family's favorite.
their biggest pride and joy.

postdoctorate fellow.
firstborn and namesake.
world traveler.

so why is it that
his eyes are so empty
when he smiles?

the summa cum laude, the 4.0 GPA,
the 12 college credits from AP testing,
the immense load of academic stress,
the studying hours after school every night,

the lead role I'd scored in our first play,
the friends I'd collected and maintained,
the retreats I'd organized and coordinated,
the chapel songs I'd practiced and performed,

all the scholarships and honors
and accomplishments and offers
and marketable skills and trophies
and leadership positions and speeches

all faded away when, diploma in hand,
I walked across that stage at 17, a year early,
looked out at the crowd, and didn't see
the person I'd done it all for.

///

Dad was "busy with work"
and "had fought traffic"
and was so terribly late that
he wasn't allowed past the foyer.

Dad handed me a flimsy laptop
while we were leaving. I knew
the real reason he'd been late was
he'd forgotten to buy it until now.

Dad promised my mom a decade ago
to give each kid a computer at graduation.
he'd spent over a thousand on the parts for eldest.
picked out middle's months in advance.

Dad boasted like he'd bent over backwards, but
from his six-figure, flex-schedule career,
he'd shelled out maybe a hundred dollars,
and taken probably ten minutes.

///

classmates with fewer merits
went to Yale, Harvard, Oxford,
got full rides to law schools,
worked for global syndicates,

but my collegiate, "genius" father,
who'd always bragged about
how smart I was, and how promising
my future and career would be,

didn't think the accolades
I'd earned my entire life
were worth more than
an afterthought.

I'd always been hurt by his absence,
and how he claimed to be proud of me.
but there was nothing he could give me
that I would have wanted in that moment.

///

afterward, I blamed myself
for wanting to have
a normal, loving dad
instead of this asshole,

and getting my hopes up
that this time would be new,
that this wouldn't be like
all the other times he'd let me down.

in all the tumult of other graduates
hugging grandmas and cousins and friends,
Dad forced an embrace and disappeared
into the crowd, abandoning me there alone.

I was left with a deep, dark hole in my chest
that told me I was such a disappointment
because I'd wanted my very best to be
enough for him to at least try.

part two

the haunting

I thought I would be free

when I stopped seeing their names
in my phone.

when the messages ceased
and I blocked their social media
and their email accounts.

when I crawled out from
underneath their grip
and away from their shadow.

I thought I would be free
for good.

now I hear them in every
thought, every word,
every mirror, every shirt,

every person, every text,
every confused look, every
moment of disturbance,

and they are loud as hell
even for them.

I desired the sky
but forgot that the cage
was from within.

the perfect crime

I doubt others believe me when I
try to explain how much I've suffered
in life. they must think I exaggerate.
I barely believe it myself.

how could such a small, soft
girl be full of such excruciating
emotional turmoil and sorrow?
it can't be possible. it can't be true.

sometimes I wish I had proof.
bruises on my arms, scars
on my face. something more
than my word, than hearsay.

I almost dream of being punched.
I want to clearly suffer, to show
on the surface how much I am
hurting--so badly, badly hurting.

but my skin is clear. my smile
is radiant. my eyes are shining.
my appetite is growing. and I am
getting very good at pretending.

I remember the second time:

I was let into the popular click
for the first time in my life.
they thought I was really funny.
I spent some time with them,
hanging out, feeling finally
accepted, no longer stranger.
then they pulled me aside
and told me I was annoying,
and to leave them alone.
the redness that consumed me
went down from head to neck.

I remember the third time:

it was a meeting of the roommates,
and all were juniors but me.
they told me my college "mom"
would be leaving in december, and so,
I was instructed to leave the apartment,
that I would be replaced with another,
closer friend. there were no hard feelings.
so I swallowed the lump in my throat.

I remember the last time:

I told them all we were like kin.
he left the group chat within seconds,
told me I was coming on too strong and
he needed space.

I reached out to a mutual friend.
"it's who you are. don't change for him,
but also he is who he is. he won't change either."
my tears ran down my chin, but I thanked him.

I remember the first time:

my dad yelled at me, screamed
at the top of his lungs that my laugh
had snapped him out of his deep focus.
I'd distracted him from his vital work,
work so important he'd come home late.
he looked at me with disdain and disgust,
something to hide away and never see again.
I nodded, and kept to the shadows after that.

I remember my mind insisting:

I am too much. I am so much that
finding less would be too simple.
I am so much that no matter how I try
to shrink, I take up the same space.
half of me wishes I could disappear.
the other half, enraged, wants to screech
from the rooftops, shout to the ceiling:

I, too, am human.

common

I don't think
it's normal
to wish
your dad had
run away
instead of
raising you.

maybe not
a good thing
to be jealous
of the family
dog for stealing
his affection.

when I told
my counselor
I was jealous
of the kids
he picked
she told me
it was common.

common and
normal are
often conflated.
but I don't feel
normal
at all. I either
feel everything
too much, or

not enough.

it burns in the
back of my throat
when I tell you
about him.
any positive
light cannot
shine.

I want to drag him
down to the mire
he made of my mind
but that's not
healthy, just
common.

I wish I could
be common.
I wish my life
were more normal.
I wish he had
cared about me
enough.

but beggars
can't be choosers.
and I can't
be a pauper
forever.

while the water heats, I

listen to a song I've heard a dozen times
and hope the lyrics consume me
that they eat away the thoughts
until they return to their nest
that they -

but I'm not like the
others, I cannot memorize lyrics with
ease, it takes
effort to ingrain them, rereading,
rereading, reciting, reciting,

over and over and still I fuck up
I fuck up
I, fuck-up.

the music is louder than the water is
louder than my husband's singing,
but all is quieter than
the shrieking
in my mind.

I singe myself with the shower,
scratch at my skin, deepen my
breaths, hold myself tight,
wishing for the grip
of terror to lessen

until it does.

and I am myself again, and I
can think again, but still,
even still, the words escape
me, then turn around and trap me,
like a ghost that recalls how to haunt.

my hands are in the controller, but
even still I run, searching for the trick
to turn the scared inside-out, to invert
it and destroy it, to regain my sanity,
and some days I find it,

but today I have lost
I have lost
I am lost.

so tired

I was seventeen the first time
my mother took me to my doctor
because of my severe exhaustion
and the nurse practitioner told me
it's not right for me to be this tired

but I didn't know why it was
that others my age burst with energy
and I drug my way through school
for the first time ever

and I didn't know
that the tired would not
go away

I have described it like a porcelain doll
with eyes that open when upright
and close when supine
except reversed

because while life makes me so tired
trying to rest simply brings to light
all my desire to get things done
and the regret that things will rot
on the counter, untouched for days

funny how the kids call it bed-rotting,
when the true rot is the world around me
a world that, without medication,
would mold and decay and rust

and expose me for the wreck
I truly am, underneath
all these covers.

scared

it's hard to believe
that some people live
without fear

that is not a life
I have ever known

I scour my brain
try to recall
a time free of panic

and only remember
other days of paranoia

my brain convulses
squeezing cherished moments
until they combust

all happiness perishes
in its grasp

how do I break out of
thoughts proven to guard
me at death's door

even as I know fear keeps
me bound to it

I'm scared of my scared
afraid to fight back
afraid to let it consume me

permanently hesitating
is all I've known

how do I detect
the absence of pain
when everything is hurting

like smelling a flower
in a burning village

even if I am the one
to arsonize my own
home?

disorganized / disoriented

I was reading the page on attachment theory
and thought I was an anxious one
until I learned that was too weak a term
for what they did to me.

no, mine was a secret fourth thing:
craving attention but fearful of receiving it,
terrified of closeness but knowing I need it,
hiding in myself while hoping someone finds me.

the trait is recognized in infants
as an irregular response to their caretakers.
the child does not know how to respond to strangers
and cannot react in a predictable way.

I imagine myself as a baby,
put in a room full of people,
unable to tell which is my parent
and unwilling to vocalize my fear.

not much has changed in that regard.
in a room full of people, I have no clue
what is acceptable or unacceptable,
kind or unkind, friendly or unfriendly.

I accept all to myself as if it is
the truest words anyone has ever
said to me. yes, even the scathing,
most disdainful insult.

because who could be more a stranger to me
than me? me, the enigma in her own
skin, scared of this existence, but
terrified of the alternative?

survivor

my surrogate Texan mother
tells me of her husband
who passed before I knew her.
he sounds like a good man.

I want to meet him,
even though it's impossible,
just to thank him
for everything he did for her.

the frustration and sadness I feel
of only knowing someone through another's eyes —
isn't that how my family views me?
when they describe me to friends, what do they say?

"I have a sister who I now know no better
than you do, full of bitterness and spite,
convinced of our err, and who we all get
along perfectly well without"

it's difficult, near incredulous, to explain
how much guilt I feel for leaving them,
though I was the one they hurt, and
being apart is for my protection.

it's a strange feeling, to grieve
family members still alive,
and even more bizarre to mourn
the family I never had,

but the worst feeling of all
is the constant gnaw of shame,
encroaching on my heart's edges,
that I wasn't strong enough to save them.

counting breaths

they taught me in therapy
to count my breaths in and out
to the beat of the box unfolding
and folding on the screen.

one, two, three, four, five,
hold, four, three, two, one,
hold.

I try to follow the pace of the box
but my mind begins to wander
almost immediately.

one. two. three. four. five.
hold, and now I'm scared
I'll never breathe again.

I know fear like my own
first name, not my last,
which wipes away to show
the trauma of my youth.

///

the longer I think,
the more I wonder
whether my suffering
was self-inflicted.

how could my mother
have known, back then,
what to do when her child
screams and cries

because breakfast was served
after she brushed her teeth,
and not before, like always?

how can you introduce fun and play
to someone so obsessive, so consumed
by rigors, that newness equates to danger?

all this time I thought my trauma
was through intention, and the thought
of it being through misinformation
crushes my mind.

///

I tell my therapist
that it is all my fault.
she explains, again,
my self-defense is faulty.

they told me I was broken
so many times for so many years
that I now spend my life
searching for what broke me.

and even if my parents had
the best intentions,
the latest resources,
the greatest strategies,

they still hurt me, so deeply,
that I forget about the knife
embedded in my psyche.

they still hurt me, so cunningly,
that I began to believe
I put the knife there myself.

they still hurt me, so sharply,
that I can feel the pain
radiating from my earliest memory,

and it is not my fault.
it is not my fault.
it is not my fault.
it is not my fault.

///

five. four. three. two. one.
hold, I chant to myself, wishing,
willing my mind to let go
of the worries forever,

but next time I am scared,
I can only recall the years
I didn't know how
to count.

after the last storm calmed
and the last rain stopped
and the last lightning ceased
and the last thunder quieted

I kept on my coat and umbrella.
the galoshes and goggles remained.
never again would I just
stand there, drenched by the elements,
seeking shelter from the onslaught
of wind and water.

the gear is so heavy, and hot
under the sun that now
and forever shines for me.

I want to take it all off, to rip off
the hazmat suit.

if only I could find the zipper.

in the twilight (dusk)

these memories that drift
in and out of my mind
that have no home

my therapist tells me
I could not process the events
so they have not been stored safely

not forgotten, but buried
a junk drawer of recollections
a liminal space of half-thoughts

one day, I claim,
I will remember it all
and set my brain on fire

but for now, the very thought
of sacrificing my mind
to reclaim my past

brings alive the embers
of obsessions
and compulsions

even speaking of this, I fear,
will spark the flames
that torture me, burn me alive

but playing with flames
in the foggy twilight -
is this the only escape route?

can I just kick it out?
can't I smother the remnants
with happy moments?

I wish this would work
but the minute I feel sadness
I feel the kindling reignite

bad habits raise their heads
as the light goes to hide:
an alter borne of dread and rumination

and as the last stroke of sunbeam
crests underneath the horizon
I feel the beast wake within.

in my childhood book of fables
is the story of Wind and Sun

Wind boasts to Sun as a man walks by
"I can make his jacket come off before you can"

Wind blows its many gusts and gales
and the man clings harder to his jacket

but Sun, instead of force, uses warmth,
and gently coaxes the gentleman into it

he takes off his jacket, sits under a tree, and rests
and Sun smiles as it shows harsh Wind

that kindness is more persuasive than fury
and people are more receptive to it

I always thought it was silly how Wind lost
and I tried to scheme ways it would have won

maybe if the angle was right, or the man was
scared enough, he would do anything Wind wanted

as fascinated as I was with the proverb,
I never thought about the lesson it taught

because I lived in Wind's grasp, buffeted back
and forth, broken into submission

in the howling of its hurricane I lived
on the ocean shore, the genteel

light and heat of Sun foreign to me
as love itself. I thought

when I finally found Sun's warmth I'd
burn, so I accepted the embrace

of Wind. decided food and shelter
were all I needed. companionship

and fulfillment weren't human. but neither
was the way Wind hurt me.

now that I know the way of Sun, I know
that I shouldn't wish for windy days, and yet

in the eye of the storm, when all I've known
is torment, how can I call Sun home?

somatism

I was never allowed to simmer,
and now I feel nothing but the scalding
fear that something has gone wrong.

maybe, my brain reasons,
if I externalize these feelings
and internalize how I react,

others will pay attention to me
for once in my dad-forsaken life
and tell me why I'm malfunctioning.

for like a broken check engine light,
my brain pings and pings warning signs
forcing me to stop everything and check.

there's never anything wrong on the surface,
but underneath my perfected exterior
is a fearful obsessive, compulsive creature.

this all-consuming monster lives in my head
and constantly screeches the worst outcome
for every situation, even impossible ones.

so I scratch my elbow, pick at my thumb, and
wash and wash my hands, hoping against hope
that something, anything will silence the alarm.

do you remember a time when you weren't afraid?
no, I do not.

do you see that the normal amount of fear is none?
no, I do not.

what are you afraid of?
being right.

why are you afraid?
being wrong.

how afraid are you?
for twenty-six years
I lived in a minefield,
and I don't know how to
stop looking for bombs.

part three

the living

anew

when I lived with mother,
I would look in the mirror
after scrubbing my hands
over and over and over

and the girl in the reflection
was unknown to me,
her focus spiraling darkly down
to the abyss within metal and glass.

now that I have grown free,
I recognize my appearance.
I can see myself in photos.
I respond to my name.

but when I look at those days,
the photos and videos taken,
all is unfamiliar, down to my teeth,
the way I hold my jaw, my speech;

strange how so many years
have been taken from me
during those two decades
of indentured servitude.

I've broken ties, but I am
less broken than ever.
open wounds turned to scars,
my greatest fears proven wrong.

my mind ever so slowly
has uncovered a new person
like a butterfly emerging
from its chrysalis

or a tadpole turned toad
leaving the murky water
for shelter and safety,
never to return

with you

I remember that fateful Christmas:
my bewildered excitement at your tenacity,
our silly conversations opening my mind
to a life that means more than mere survival.

right when I thought you'd vanish,
there you were in my messages with me.
with time, we moved to watching television
and complaining about my mom's cooking.

that one winter's night, you watched me.
you weren't talking, weren't touching, weren't moving,
just looked into my eyes as we sat on my dorm bed.
I started to trust you wouldn't leave, then.

now I trust you more than anyone I've known,
more than I ever thought was possible.
no one knows me like you do,
not even myself.

every day, I'm grateful
that you stay by my side,
not only in the hard times,
but in the dull ones too—

the ones where we wake up late
and drag ourselves out of bed
and go to the local cafe and talk
about finances and the future.

I know I'll always have you,
and that even once we're old,
I'll still be telling you bad jokes,
just to hear you sigh at me

one more time.

I've watched shows about the kindness of strangers,
marveled at how regular people had the power
to heal and help those in need.

all I had known thus far
was how little power I had
to help anyone, especially myself,

until I met my own stranger:
a gruff, angry man who saved me
when I froze on the road in fear.

he was just like the others,
I'd reasoned, and would take advantage
of my cluelessness and naivety;

but he guided me to a side street,
apologized for being harsh,
admitted to being scared.

I didn't know how to respond to it,
to his generosity and vulnerability, such that
even my own family couldn't, wouldn't, give me, but

the stranger's mercy dug into my walls,
rooted into my heart, and sprouted
bursts of hope through my mind.

I took a deep breath.
I released my clutch on control,
the painful-tight grip that had steered me astray
and trusted my guardian angel not to falter.

things I know without asking

his favorite drink at all our favorite stops
what local Tex-Mex restaurant he likes
to set his clothes out after he showers

how to make him laugh
where he is ticklish
not to tickle him, or else

how he likes to be held
that I am his favorite person
that he will never abandon me

what makes him upset
what words wound him
what brings him great sorrow

that he is the best part of my life
he is worth putting down my weapons
he deserves my trust

how he has all the power to hurt me
how I have all the power to hurt him
how easy it would be to give up

and that he would never,
ever,
ever hurt me.

no matter what.

between the boughs

I used to wander through my arboretum,
and I'd quickly lose myself in the leaves.
there was so much to see here, to smell.
I'd wander the winding trails.

I locked my gate, climbed up the trees,
memorized the paths, walked them
over and over, preserving old habits
to keep peace in a world of chaos.

after decades, the peace became a prison.
those trees turned inward, closed-in, bare.
I didn't want out of my forest just yet,
but I wished I had someone to help me.

///

someone knocks on the rotting
wood of my orchard's gate. I peek
through the spokes to spy a man
who had once caught my eye.

surprised, I venture from my containment
and we walk down a gravel path together.
he waves me over into his greenhouse,
full of warmth and love and light.

I balk at its simplicity, but marvel
when I move closer to the flowers and
sense a complexity beyond what
lies on the surface. it astonishes me.

he asks me if he can visit my orchard.
I don't want him to. all I can recall
are the thorns and thistles, and how
overgrown the path has become.

not that I've abandoned caring for it.
I spend all my time tending for these trees.
I just don't know—have never known—*how*.
and there hasn't been a guest for a long, long time.

///

I decide to let the stranger in, and he
doesn't scowl at the barren branches.
he doesn't balk at the thick brambles
growing near the center, either.

instead, he treats me like it's…fine.
not an "embarrassment," or a "freak," or a "failure."
he listens to my struggles, denies my self-hatred.
he says I didn't, couldn't, have known better.

in his eyes are neither compassion nor anger.
instead, they're filled with something else,
something I've only seen glimpses of,
only when I've been very obedient. not like this.

///

the gentle stranger shows me a flower
while he teaches me how to garden:
a rose, its petals bursting with vibrancy,
thorns prickling down its stem.

his grandmother taught him husbandry

from when he was very young, he tells me.
he prunes a few buds with a pair of worn shears,
explains that trimming it helps the plant heal.

and I think I, too, am beginning to heal
while watching his gentle pruning.
for the first time in my solitary life,
I want this guest to visit every day.

in the twilight (dawn)

as the sun rises
I let it shine on the pain
of my past

I know that come sunset
it will have flooded back into me
like a ghoul taking hold

but in the mornings I can be free
at peace
not having a worry of their clutches

in the night I dream
of the ways they've hurt me
and I wake up exhausted

they drain my energy
without saying a word
for five years

but as daylight peeks over the horizon
my dark journey through rumination
comes to a close

in the twilight
I can make out more mile markers -
a hiking trail up the summit-less climb

I title the mountain "healing" with affection,
though the journey has been anything but,
full of bruises, gashes, bloodied knees

all the pain of nightfall fades away when
strips of light sneaking through the treetops
illumine how far I have come

and the best part of all is when I look beside me,
feel your hand in mine, and once again
realize I've never walked alone

as a child, I clung to this white blanket
and its lace ruffles. I'd carry it like Linus,
pet the soft fuzzy texture, and over and
over and over trace the pattern
until the world no longer hurt me.
yet mother hid the blanket

and told me I could live without, so
I didn't see it again for many years.
I soon replaced it with a stuffed animal
dog, nicknamed "Doggy," who I carried
with me everywhere - supermarket, church;

where I went, there he was, looking at me
with warm brown eyes and russet fur,
wondering where our next adventure
would take us. I savored the small moments
of just me and him against the world.
no one could keep us apart, but mother

told me I needed to be brave. and I tried,
slowly, going from one outing apart to two,
until Doggy joined my hundred-fold collection
of stuffies that took up space in my closet, never
to be caressed or held or loved again, until

you showed up, and you loved me.
you walked with me and guarded me,
told me I didn't need to be brave
by myself anymore. it wasn't just me
against the world, and you held me,
and I learned it would be ok

to trust you. I didn't have to feel
guilty, or self-conscious, or embarrassed.
I could adventure again, journey into the depths
of terror with my security blanket in clutch.
you were my safe place, but mother tried

to make me see you as a threat, see a red thread
through the blanket that had done nothing but
warm me. I realized then who the real threat was,
the one who had stolen away my safety
all this time, keeping me miserable.
mom was a sea of uncertainty, and you

didn't take her away from me. no,
you said I could stay, but I know
how much she sought my ruin.
I can see that her blanket is stained
scarlet from all the wounds she has

given me in the name of protection.
she wanted so badly to be my security
blanket. instead, all she gave me was
a blanket view of my insecurities,
every shortcoming on great display.
I gave up my last attachment to her

and chose to listen to you, the one
who has always sought my benefit,
the one who sets me free from fear.
you ask me if I'm ready to go with you.
and with you at my side, I am.

my way out, ii

now that I've
made my roost,
I catch glimpses
of my old cage
in the corners
of my eyes.

when I feel the bars,
even though they're gone,
I'm flighty, easily ruffled,
biting, tearing down,
and I'm afraid—

it happens often,
so, so often,
almost all day,
almost every day.

but fighting back,
clawing at those bars,
avoiding everything
that reminds me
of my old self,

brought me nothing
but tired wings,
empty claws, and
a deep longing
for somewhere
to call home.

the roost is safe.
I say once more:
my roost is safe,
I am not in danger,
no one here waits
for my downfall.

no one will
force me to go
where I don't
belong or fit in
ever, ever,
ever again.

I meet my mind
right there. when it
misses the cage,
I tell myself
that it's natural.

I have to grasp
that it's okay
to grieve places
and not want to
go back to them.

I have to forgive
my own mind
for being scared
of loved ones
only here to help.

who knew that,
even after I
escape the cage,
I must accept
the hurt it left?

now I know
my way out
of their cage
couldn't be
a single choice,
but a hundred
tiny resolutions,
each and every hour,
to stay, to stay,
to stay.

pain is easy.
pain is easy to feel.
pain is easy to get.

pain is the route I've taken
through my mind a hundred times,
tail tucked between my legs.

pain is the waves of fear I feel
when I assume their "no" is to me,
and not to what I wanted.

pain is a great bubbling mire.
the more I struggle, the faster
I sink into the sorrowful dark.

pain is a consistent reminder
of the wounds I had before,
and the bandages I needed.

pain is nothing but scar tissue now,
but the tissue keeps me from healing,
and surgery only does so much, so

pain is motivation to do therapy,
to learn how to move despite the scars,
and with them, and around them.

pain is a part of life, not all of it.
pain is a reminder of who I was.
pain is a sign of how far I've come.

pain isn't my enemy, but instead
a tool my body used to keep me safe.
pain warded me from getting hurt again.

pain is hard.
pain is hard to see.
pain is hard to let go.

over and over I talk to pain.
I thank pain for protecting me,
and I release pain from that burden.

and after a long time, I am now
okay with feeling like everything
is going to hurt me again.

I embrace the possibility of hurt
alongside the potential of hope.
I accept the mixed bag life gives me.

pain still hurts a lot, but I don't
think about pain much anymore.
I let pain flow past like logs in a river.

I have pain.
I feel pain. I see pain.
I get pain. I let go of pain.

I think about pain not being easy or hard,
good or bad, evil or kind, but just
being. just like life.

just like me.

re-parenting

people ask me why I don't have kids
I tell them it's not for me

they say I won't know unless I try
but truth is, I've been a mom before

a new mother at 16, I'd help my child out of bed
fix her lunch, send her off to work after school

we co-slept in my bed the first few months
then separate, close by, her mattress in my room

I'd listen to her struggles, meet her needs
and shrink my own as much as I could

until I was lost in the process
and put my purpose aside

but once I moved out for college
and left my child behind

I couldn't make my own decisions
because I'd never learned how

///

when people ask me why I don't have kids
I don't know how to explain

that I've been a mom before
but my child is far older than me

my child gave birth to me
my child taught me to walk

but that one October night,
she wouldn't take back her title

and now, after becoming a parent,
caretaking has become second nature

I tell myself how it's okay to have less
to want less, to need less, to be less

and it took over a decade to realize
I don't like who she made me to be

///

people ask me why I don't have kids
but because I've been a mom before

I know that it is not for me
to bring new life into the world

to nurture the growth of a malleable being
and hold their hand while they form who they are

to cater to their needs, but let them fail on their own
to teach them of life's limits, but show them its potential

so instead I am parenting myself
I show me it's okay to desire, to grow

that it's okay to seek safety in others
instead of always giving it away

I find my inner child and raise her well
she makes me laugh, knows how to have fun

she sparks with excitement and passion and drive
reignites my desire to have a fulfilling life

we blow the dust off of my purpose
to find who I am for the very first time

///

so when people ask me why I don't have kids
and say I won't know unless I try

I say, I decide who I want to be.
and no one can take that choice away.

successful

as a kid I hoped I'd be powerful.
I'd walk down the hallway
of some giant convention center,

wearing a black blazer
with a matching pencil skirt
and a suit jacket with the shoulder pads.

now that I'm an adult, I am powerful.
but the power has changed.
I don't even own a blazer.

I don't look the same, or talk like I did.
I don't care what I do for a living,
though I take pride in my work.

but here I am at the card shop,
begging my husband to treat himself
because I love him more than life.

here I am playing with my cats
and thinking about trading card prices
and writing poetry about the pain.

I am powerful, but the power isn't the same.
the power isn't in comparison to others.
it isn't in money or career ladders.

it's in investment of action:
not its depth, but its constancy,
a leaky faucet slowly filling a sink.

it's in love and adoration.
it's in protecting my peace
and great willingness to change.

and now, I am the kind woman
I've always wanted to be my friend.
that is where my power lies.

I'm late

the trouble with an adult diagnosis
is finding all the great coping skills
don't work on you like they should.

I count my breaths in and out.
hold for so many seconds.
I lost count. I count wrong. I start over.

I hold my breath for three counts.
I start to panic—or think I do,
but the panic is always there.

see, mom planted worry seeds in my brain,
and dad watered them as I grew up,
and now the fear is everywhere.

I can see the roots clearly, but
I don't know how to rip them up
without destroying myself in the process.

so I learn to live with it.
I obsess. I compulse. I disorder
until I'm so scared I can't move.

there's nothing I can do to run away.
my only safe place is in flames.
I can't give up now. I won't.

I can't put down the matches.
but I can put out the fire.
I can learn to put them out faster.

I count my breaths in and out.
I thank myself for breathing,
thank my lungs for functioning.

forgive my old self for
burning it all down
to keep me warm.

and accept that the smoke
is not my fault, and that
no one wants to hurt me.

I'm late, but I'm still here.
though my mind fights me,
I'll fight back 'til the day I die.

acknowledgements

Sam Owen, thank you for the gorgeous artwork on this cover.
B. E. Evans, huge thanks for the smashing cover design yet again.
Thank you to my cheerleaders, in all the different parts of my life:
Micah, James, Mark, Chuck, Courtney, Meesh, Zero, Jorban, Sarah D,
Sarah L, Marissa, Nick, Dana, Allison, Steven, Jordan, Anna, Miranda C,
Katie, Miranda M, Jennifer, Natalie, Laura, Dax, Melanie, Alexis, Trina,
Ruthie, Choyce, Amanda, Jami, Eddie, Chris, and all the Laurens.
Thank you Big Back Wednesday crew for cheering me up without fail.
Gigantic thanks to Crazy Four Books & Coffee, where the majority of
this book was written.
Jacob, I love you so much. we are each other's better halves, and I'm
forever grateful to you. Charles, and Amber, thank you for taking me
in under your guiding wings.
Hazel, thank you for listening to my unending rants in the process.
And to you, my reader: thank you for continuing to pick up my books.
I appreciate you, and I hope you enjoyed this one too.